Vocabulary Booster

for Cambridge English Qualifications

A1 MOVERS

How to use this book

Introduction

Team Together Vocabulary Boosters are designed to be a fun and engaging way of consolidating and extending vocabulary from the *Team Together* series. Each Vocabulary Booster includes 10 units, based around a different topic relevant to children and their lives. The books also offer support for children preparing for the Cambridge English Qualifications for young learners.

Vocabulary presentation

In the first part of each unit, key vocabulary is introduced in the context of a large, colourful scene, which will engage children and spark their curiosity. Children are encouraged to explore the scene through a series of short activities and accompanying audio.

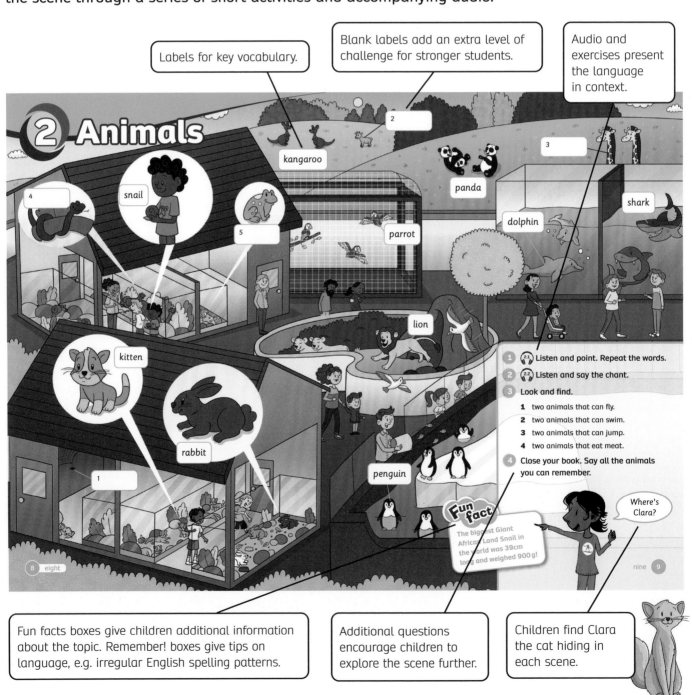

Labels for key vocabulary.

Blank labels add an extra level of challenge for stronger students.

Audio and exercises present the language in context.

Fun facts boxes give children additional information about the topic. Remember! boxes give tips on language, e.g. irregular English spelling patterns.

Additional questions encourage children to explore the scene further.

Children find Clara the cat hiding in each scene.

Vocabulary practice

In the second part of each unit, there are two pages of activities which provide further consolidation and practice of the vocabulary through a variety of fun activities.

Vocabulary practised through reading and listening tasks.

Target icons identify Cambridge English Qualifications style tasks.

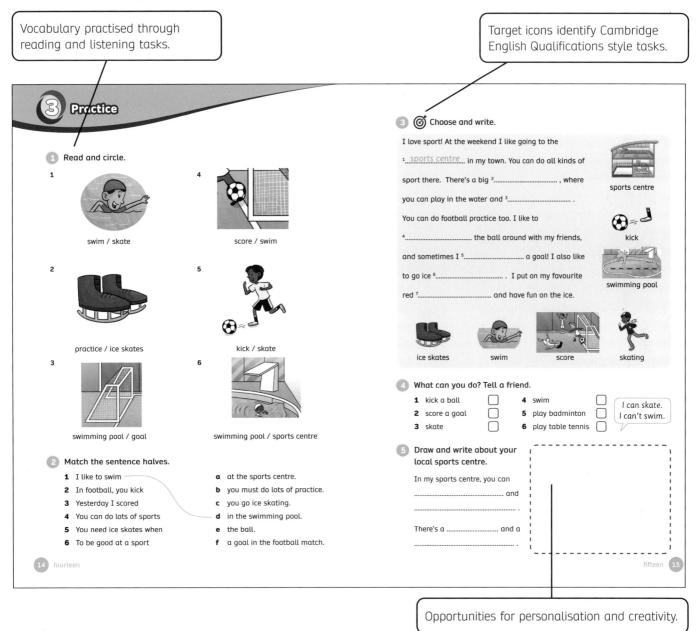

Opportunities for personalisation and creativity.

Other books in the series

There are three Vocabulary Booster books in the *Team Together* series, each one relating to one of the Cambridge English Qualifications for young learners tests:

- Pre A1 Starters

- A1 Movers

- A2 Flyers

We suggest that you use the Vocabulary Booster for Cambridge English Qualifications A2 Movers with *Team Together* Levels 3 and 4.

Our final tip for using this book? Have fun!

1 My house

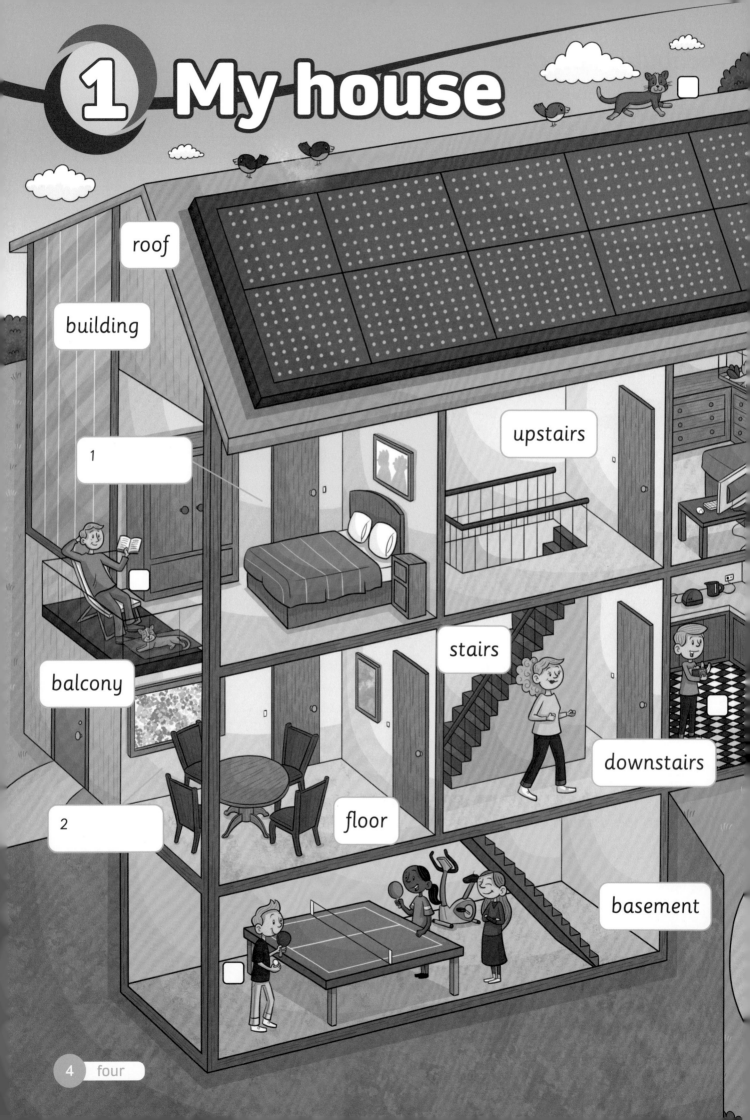

roof

building

1

balcony

2

upstairs

stairs

floor

downstairs

basement

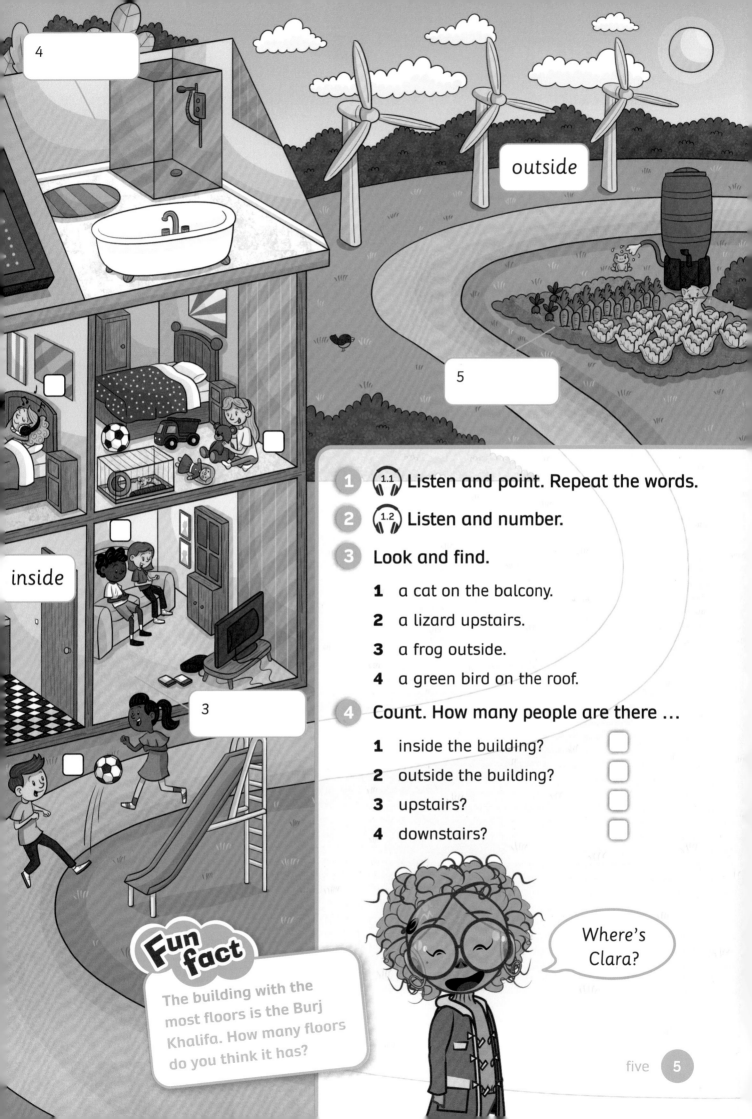

4

outside

5

inside

3

1 🎧(1.1) **Listen and point. Repeat the words.**

2 🎧(1.2) **Listen and number.**

3 **Look and find.**

1 a cat on the balcony.

2 a lizard upstairs.

3 a frog outside.

4 a green bird on the roof.

4 **Count. How many people are there ...**

1 inside the building? ☐

2 outside the building? ☐

3 upstairs? ☐

4 downstairs? ☐

Where's Clara?

Fun fact

The building with the most floors is the Burj Khalifa. How many floors do you think it has?

1 Practice

1 🎯 🎧 1.3 Listen and tick.

1 Where is Daisy?

a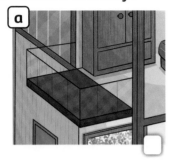

b

c

2 Who's playing outside?

a

b

c

3 Which room is upstairs?

a

b

c

2 Write the words.

1 r _ _ f

2 u p s t a i r s

3 i _ _ i _ _

4 b _ _ c _ _ y

5 o _ _ s _ _ e

6 b _ d _ _ _ _

7 s _ _ _ r _

8 b _ _ _ m _ _ _

3 Read and write *Yes* or *No*.

1 He's in the basement. ....*Yes*....

2 He's inside the building. ....

3 They're playing outside. ....

4 The girl is on the balcony. ....

5 They are on the roof. ....

6 The mouse is upstairs. ....

4 Design your own building. Answer the questions.

1 How many floors has your building got? ....

2 What rooms are on each floor? ....

3 Is there a basement? ....

4 Are there any balconies? ....

5 What is there outside your building? ....

5 Describe your building to a friend.

It's got ... rooms.

The ... is on the ground floor.

There's ...

2 Animals

kangaroo

snail

4

5

kitten

rabbit

1

2

panda

3

shark

dolphin

parrot

lion

penguin

1 🎧 2.1 Listen and point. Repeat the words.

2 🎧 2.2 Listen and say the chant.

3 Look and find.

   1 two animals that can fly.

   2 two animals that can swim.

   3 two animals that can jump.

   4 two animals that eat meat.

4 Close your book. Say all the animals you can remember.

Fun fact

The biggest Giant African Land Snail in the world was 39cm long and weighed 900g!

Where's Clara?

2 Practice

1 Find the animals. Write the words.

1

......dolphin......

5

....

6

....

7

....

2

....

8

....

s	h	a	r	k	t	i	k	r	t	q
a	t	y	u	i	a	p	i	a	r	k
q	d	p	a	n	d	a	t	b	b	a
z	o	x	p	k	g	m	t	b	p	n
s	l	c	a	s	r	d	e	i	p	g
n	p	t	r	w	t	e	n	t	w	a
a	h	v	r	i	u	v	b	n	q	r
i	i	b	o	y	l	i	o	n	z	o
l	n	h	t	h	j	b	z	m	w	o
r	f	m	p	e	n	g	u	i	n	h

3

....

9

....

4

....

10

....

2 (2.3) Which is different? Circle and say why. Then listen.

1

2

3

3 Read and write the animal.

1

I like eating leaves.
I'm black and white.
I live in China.
I'm a ....*panda*.............. .

4

I like eating fish.
I can walk on two feet.
I can swim very well.
I'm a ....

2

I can jump quickly.
I'm brown.
I live in Australia.
I'm a ....

5

I'm grey.
I like eating fish.
I can swim and jump out of
   the water.
I'm a ....

3

I like eating meat.
I can run quickly.
I've got big teeth.
I'm a ....

6

I've got wings and feathers.
I can fly and talk.
I'm red, green yellow and blue.
I'm a ....

4 Choose an animal. Draw and write your own fact file.

1 This is a

....

2 It's

....

3 It's got

....

4 It can

....

5 Describe your animal to a friend.

It's got ...   It can ...   Is it a ...?

3 At the sports centre

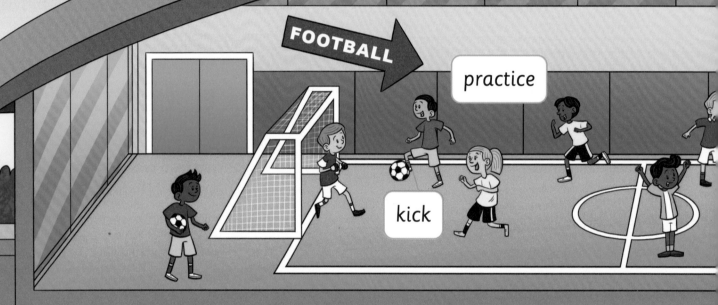

sports centre

FOOTBALL

practice

kick

ice skates

skate

swimming pool

ice skating

swim

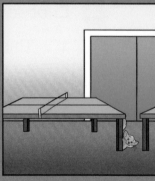

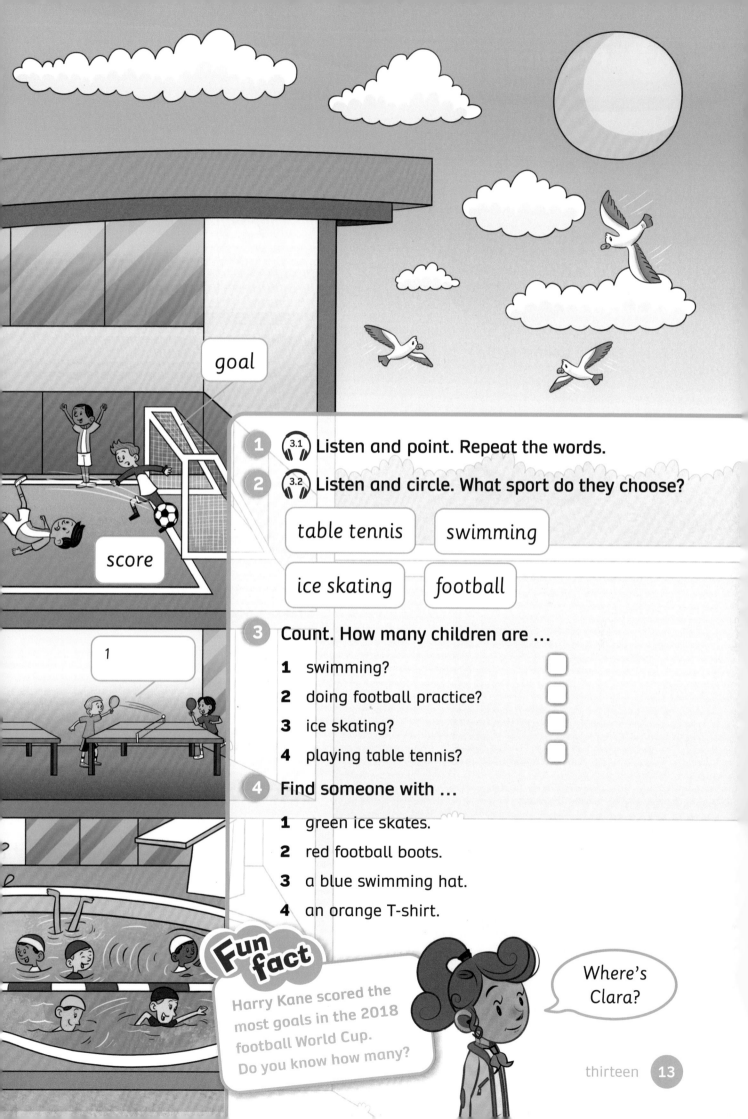

goal

score

1

1 🎧 3.1 **Listen and point. Repeat the words.**

2 🎧 3.2 **Listen and circle. What sport do they choose?**

| table tennis | swimming |

| ice skating | football |

3 **Count. How many children are ...**

1 swimming?
2 doing football practice?
3 ice skating?
4 playing table tennis?

4 **Find someone with ...**

1 green ice skates.
2 red football boots.
3 a blue swimming hat.
4 an orange T-shirt.

Fun fact

Harry Kane scored the most goals in the 2018 football World Cup. Do you know how many?

Where's Clara?

1 **Read and circle.**

1

swim / skate

4

score / swim

2

practice / ice skates

5

kick / skate

3

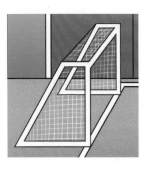

swimming pool / goal

6

swimming pool / sports centre

2 **Match the sentence halves.**

1 I like to swim

2 In football, you kick

3 Yesterday I scored

4 You can do lots of sports

5 You need ice skates when

6 To be good at a sport

a at the sports centre.

b you must do lots of practice.

c you go ice skating.

d in the swimming pool.

e the ball.

f a goal in the football match.

3 🎯 Choose and write.

I love sport! At the weekend I like going to the

¹ _sports centre_ in my town. You can do all kinds of

sport there. There's a big ² .... , where

you can play in the water and ³ ....

You can do football practice too. I like to

⁴ .... the ball around with my friends,

and sometimes I ⁵ .... a goal! I also like

to go ice ⁶ .... I put on my favourite

red ⁷ .... and have fun on the ice.

sports centre

kick

swimming pool

ice skates   swim   score   skating

4 **What can you do? Tell a friend.**

1 kick a ball ☐   4 swim ☐
2 score a goal ☐   5 play badminton ☐
3 skate ☐   6 play table tennis ☐

I can skate.
I can't swim.

5 **Draw and write about your local sports centre.**

In my sports centre, you can

.... and

....

There's a .... and a

....

invite

WE INVITE YOU TO THE CIRCUS

4

grandson

grandparent

clown

1  **4.1** Listen and point. Repeat the words.

2 **4.2** Listen and say the chant.

3 Can you find a clown with …

   1 a blue hat?

   2 a red ball?

   3 orange shoes?

   4 green hair?

4 Count. How many … are there?

   1 purple balloons ☐

   2 yellow balloons ☐

   3 pink balloons ☐

   4 white balloons ☐

How many balloons are there in total?

Fun fact

There were clowns in Ancient Roman times. They wore pointed hats, and they were funny!

Where's Clara?

4 Practice

1  4.3 Listen and circle.

1 a

b

2 a

b

3 a

b

4 a

b

2 Find and circle. Then choose and write.

auntdaughterson(grandson)granddaughterunclegrandparents

1 This is my grandmother. I'm her <u>grandson</u> . My sister is her ....

2 My grandmother and grandfather are my ....

3 My mum's sister is my ....

4 My dad's brother is my ....

5 My sister is my mum's ....

6 This is my mum. I'm her ....

18 eighteen

3 Read and circle.

Last night I went to the [1] **clown / circus**.
My mum [2] **invited / enjoyed** some of my
family and friends! My [3] **grandparents
/ granddaughter** were there. I was so
happy to see them. My mum's sister, my
[4] **uncle / aunt**, was there too. All the children
enjoyed the circus. My mum and the other
[5] **grandsons / grown-ups** enjoyed it too.
I loved the [6] **clowns / sons** – they were funny.
One of them gave me a pink balloon.

4 Draw and write about a day out with your family.

1 Where did you go?

....

....

2 What did you do?

....

....

3 Who did you invite?

....

....

4 Did you have fun?

....

....

5 Tell your friend about your day out.

I went to the …   I invited …   We …

5 A picnic

hide

picnic

1

cup

glass

bowl

blanket

milkshake

lake

bottle

2

plate

4

3

5

1 **5.1** Listen and point. Repeat the words.

2 **5.2** Listen and say the chant.

3 Find someone who is …

… swimming in the lake.

… fishing.

… eating a sandwich.

… catching a ball.

… hiding

4 What food or drink can you see …

1 in a bowl?

2 in a glass?

3 in a cup?

4 on a plate?

5 in a bottle?

Fun fact
Did you know? Picnics first started in France. People enjoyed eating outside in parks.

Where's Clara?

Practice

1 Complete the crossword.

bottle   picnic   lake   hide   blanket   bowl   milkshake   plate

3

6

5

2

4 down

4 across

1

7

2 Write the correct word in each sentence.

1 I like drinking chocolate ....   salad   banana   milkshake

2 I can't see you! Where are
you .... ?   singing   talking   hiding

3 There's a .... of water on the table.   plate   bottle   box

4 At a picnic, people sit on a ....   blanket   table   bed

5 Susan ate some food from a ....   lake   bowl   bottle

6 The children like swimming
in the ....   hill   lake   mountain

3  **Listen and tick.**

1 Where did Jim go at the weekend?

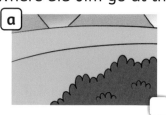 **a**

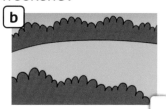 **b**

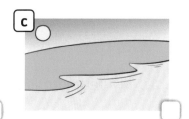 **c**

2 What did Jim eat at the picnic?

a

b

c

3 What was Jim's favourite drink?

a

b

c

4 What games did Jim play?

a

b

c

4 **Draw and write about a picnic.**

1 Where is your picnic?

2 What is there to eat and drink?

3 What sports do you play?

My picnic is at the ....

There's .... and

.... to eat.

There's .... and

.... to drink.

We're ....

5 **Describe your picnic to a friend.**

My picnic is on the beach.

There's ...

We're ...

Review 1

1 Write the words.

1 My bedroom is u p s t a i r s .

2 The bathroom is on the first _ _ _ _ _ _ .

3 I like playing football _ _ _ _ _ _ _ _ .

4 The kitchen isn't upstairs. It's _ _ _ _ _ _ _ _ _ _ _ .

5 Don't climb on the _ _ _ _ !

6 This room is under the ground;
it's the _ _ _ _ _ _ _ _ .

| patrisus |
| olfor |
| setuodi |
| swodanirst |
| orof |
| stebname |

2 Look and write the animals.

1

rabbit

2

3

4

5

6

3 Circle the correct word in each sentence.

1 You can **swim / skate** in the swimming pool.

2 You can play badminton at the **shopping / sports** centre.

3 In basketball, you don't **kick / throw** the ball.

4 In football, you must **win / score** a goal.

5 You must wear ice **boots / skates** for ice skating.

6 I do football **practice / score** every day.

4 (R1.1) **Listen and draw lines.**

Charlie

Lily

Julia

Daisy

Fred

5 **Choose and write.**

bowl plate ~~picnic~~ milkshake lake blanket bottles cup hide

Today we're eating outside. We're having a ¹..........*picnic*.......... .

We're sitting on a big ²................................. . We're next to a ³................................. .

There's a big ⁴................................. of sandwiches on the picnic table and

there are two ⁵................................. of lemonade. I don't like lemonade so I'm

drinking a strawberry ⁶................................. . It's delicious! My dad is eating a

big ⁷................................. of salad. My mum is drinking a ⁸................................. .

of coffee. My brothers and sisters are playing a game of ⁹.................................

and seek.

Picnics are fun!

asleep

awake

get up

get dressed

16

18

1

bus stop

3

get on

get undressed

wake up

wash

get off

20

2

1 6.1 Listen and point. Repeat the words.

2 6.2 Listen and number.

3 Say the colour of the house where ...

1 children are sleeping.

2 a woman is wearing pyjamas.

3 a boy is reading a book.

4 a cat is on the balcony.

4 Count. How many ... ?

1 people are at the bus stop

2 people are on the bus

3 people are riding a bike

4 people are sleeping

5 birds are on the roof

Fun fact

Did you know that people spend one third of their life sleeping? Cats spend 12–16 hours each day asleep.

Where's Clara?

1 Look and choose.

1

get dressed / get undressed

2

awake / asleep

3

get up / wash

4

get on / bus stop

5

get off / wake up

2 🎧 6.3 Number the sentences in order. Listen to check your answers.

a I get off the bus and walk into school. ☐

b I go downstairs and I say goodbye to my mum. ☐

c I walk to the bus stop and I get on the bus. ☐

d Every morning, I wake up at 7 o'clock. ☐ 1

e I go back to my bedroom and I get dressed. ☐

f I get up and go to the bathroom. ☐

g I wash my hands and face. ☐

3 Read and match.

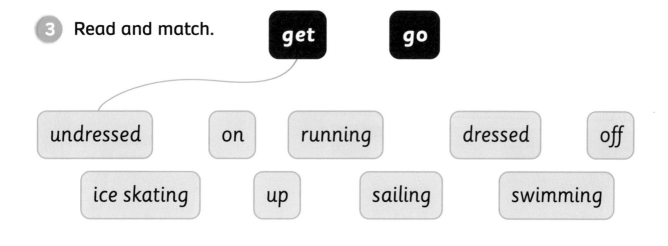

get   **go**

undressed   on   running   dressed   off

ice skating   up   sailing   swimming

4 Now complete the text. Use the words and phrases from this lesson.

MY WEEK

On school days, I ¹...........wake........... up at 7 o'clock.

Then I ²............................... up and I ³............................... dressed.

After breakfast, I walk to the bus ⁴............................... .

I get ⁵............................... the bus and travel to school.

I get ⁶............................... the bus outside the school.

In the evening, I ⁷............................... undressed and I go to bed.

I'm always tired so I'm usually ⁸............................... before 9 o'clock.

At weekends, I get ⁹............................... late. I ¹⁰............................... swimming at the

swimming pool. On Sundays I go ¹¹............................... on the lake.

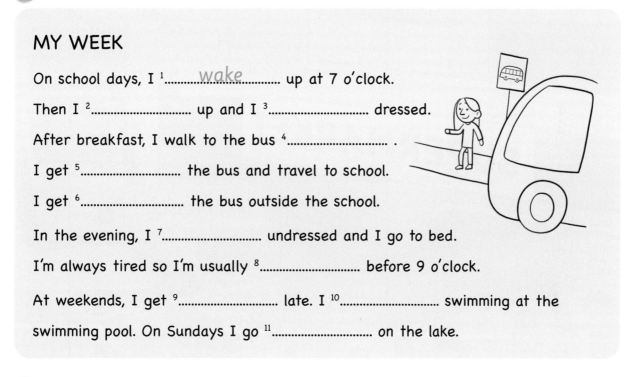

5 Draw and write about your day.

In the morning I ....

and I ....

In the evening I ....

and I ....

7 A modern town

DVD

I'm at the bus station. Where are you?

send

1

I'm in the supermarket.

text message

SUPERMARKET

MOBILE PHONE / TABLET

comic book

app

pop star

bus station

laptop

2

town centre

My story

e-book

1 🎧 7.1 **Listen and point. Repeat the words.**

2 🎧 7.2 **Listen and number.**

3 **Name five things you can buy in the supermarket.**

4 **Count. How many … are there?**

1 people in the town centre ☐
2 cups in the café ☐
3 laptops in the café ☐
4 buses in the bus station ☐

Fun fact

Did you know? People around the world send more than 18.5 billion text messages every month!

Where's Clara?

1 Match the words and pictures.

1	bus		centre ⓐ		i
2	pop		book ⓑ		ii
3	town		message ⓒ		iii
4	comic		star ⓓ		iv
5	lap		top ⓔ		v
6	text		station ⓕ		vi

2 🎯 Read and write the words.

1 There are lots of shops and cafés in this place. ...... *town centre* ......

2 This is a small computer that you can carry with you. ....

3 It's a book that you read on a tablet. ....

4 It's a place where you wait for a bus. ....

5 They help you play games on your mobile phone. ....

6 You can use this to watch a film. ....

7 This person can sing and dance. ....

3 Listen and circle the words.

Hi Sally. Do you want to go to the ¹**bus station / town centre**?

Yes good idea! I want to buy the new Serena ²**DVD / comic book**. She's my favourite ³**teacher / pop star**.

Ok. Let's meet at the ⁴**bus stop / café**.

Great. I'll bring my ⁵**laptop / e-book** so we can play some games.

Cool! ⁶**Send / bring** me a ⁷**text / app** message when you're there.

4 Answer the questions.

1 Who's your favourite pop star? ....

2 Have you got a laptop? ....

3 Do you prefer reading comic books or e-books? ....

4 Can you send a text message? ....

5 How often do you go to the town centre? ....

6 Do you like watching DVDs? ....

  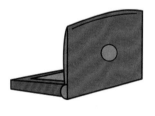 

5 Now ask a partner the questions from activity 4. Tell them your answers.

Have you got a laptop?

No, but I've got a computer.

8 In the countryside

field

bat

farm

farmer

1

2

3

fly

5

sky

tractor

countryside

sheep

plant

4

grass

1 8.1 Listen and point. Repeat the words.

2 8.2 Listen and say the chant.

3 Can you find a … ?

   1 yellow baby duck

   2 brown cow

   3 white mouse

   4 black sheep

4 Count. How many … are there?

1 bats	☐	**4** chickens	☐
2 kittens	☐	**5** cows	☐
3 sleeping cats	☐	**6** horses	☐

Fun fact

A baby horse is a foal. A baby bat is a pup. Do you know words for other baby farm animals?

Where's Clara?

8 Practice

1 Find and circle. Write the words.

1

countryside

5

....

6

....

2

....

3

....

4

....

c	o	u	n	t	r	y	s	i	d	e
a	t	y	u	i	o	p	i	a	b	p
q	d	b	a	t	t	s	k	y	g	q
z	p	x	p	a	n	d	a	r	r	y
f	l	t	r	a	c	t	o	r	a	p
i	a	f	r	o	g	e	d	h	s	d
e	n	v	r	i	u	v	b	n	s	p
l	t	f	a	r	m	e	r	e	o	e
d	n	h	t	h	j	b	z	m	o	y
r	f	m	p	e	n	f	l	y	n	b

7

....

8

....

9

....

2 🎯 (8.3) Listen and write.

At the Farm

1 Farmer's name: J.........................

2 Number of fields: ....

3 Colour of tractor: ....

4 What's in the fields?:

animals and ....

5 Farmer's favourite animal:

....

3 Read and match.

Town **Countryside** **Both**

town centre field tractor kitten farmer

street fly sky bat trees bus station

4 Choose and write.

1 I don't live in the town. I live in the ....

plant | countryside

2 My pet cat has five little ....

bats | kittens

3 Look at the sun up in the ....

sky | grass

4 A .... works with animals.

doctor | farmer

5 These small black animals fly around at night.
They're ....

bats | cows

6 A farmer drives a .... in the fields.

tractor | bus

5 Draw and write about the countryside.

In the countryside, there are

.... and ....

There's a .... and a

....

6 Ask and answer with a friend.

What's in the countryside?

There are plants and animals ...

9 At the hospital

doctor

1

2

3

fall

4

headache

cough

lift (elevator)

seat

hospital

toothache

dentist

frightened

nurse

1 (9.1) Listen and point. Repeat the words.

2 (9.2) Listen and number.

3 Find someone who ...

... is eating a sandwich.

... is sitting on a brown seat.

... is talking to a nurse.

... is waiting for a lift.

4 Count. How many ... are there in the picture?

1 nurses

2 doctors

3 dentists

4 children

RECEPTION

Remember!

lift / elevator

Where's Clara?

9 Practice

1 Reorder the letters. Write the words.

1 o d c r o t

.......doctor.......

2 s t e d i n t

....

3 s e r u n

....

4 t i s o l p a h

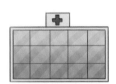

....

5 l a l f

....

6 t a s e

....

7 f l i t

....

8 a h o c t o t h e

....

9 h u c o g

....

2 Read. Circle the best answer.

1 Doctors and nurses work

   a at the sports centre.

   b at the hospital.

2 I've got toothache.

   a You need to see the dentist.

   b You need to see a doctor.

3 My grandma can't walk up the stairs.

   a She should run.

   b She should take the lift.

4 Be careful up that tree!

   a Don't get up!

   b Don't fall!

5 We saw a big snake at the zoo.

   My little sister was

   a frightened.

   b boring.

6 I'm tired. Can I …

   a stand on the chair?

   b sit on this seat?

3  Complete the dialogues. Then listen and check.

seats   cough   nurses   headache   lift   frightened   ~~hospital~~

Good morning. Welcome to City
¹.....Hospital..... . Can I help you?

Yes, I've got a ²..................... and a
³..................... . I need to see the doctor.

Alright. Please take the
⁴..................... to the first floor.
Then sit on one of the blue
⁵..................... and wait.

Don't worry. The doctors and
⁶..................... here are all very kind!

It's OK mum, I like hospitals.
I'm not ⁷..................... .

4 Answer the questions for you.

1 Have you ever been to a hospital? When / Why?..

2 Have you ever had toothache?..

3 Have you ever fallen in the street?..

4 Do you usually walk upstairs or take the lift?.......................................

5 Do you ever feel frightened? When? ....

5 Now ask and answer with a friend.

Have you ever
been to a hospital?

Yes, I visited my grandma
in hospital last week.

10 The weather

cloud

sunny

1

cloudy

1

rainbow

2

3

wind

windy

ice

snow

weather

rain

wet

1 (10.1) **Listen and point. Repeat the words.**

2 (10.2) **Listen and say the number.**

3 **Find and circle.**

1 a grandma with her granddaughter.

2 a girl flying a kite.

3 a snowman in the snow.

4 a girl swimming.

5 a child falling on the ice.

4 **Find someone wearing …**

… a yellow scarf.

… an orange coat.

… purple shorts.

… a red sweater.

Fun fact

Did you know? Antarctica is one of the windiest places on Earth. At night, you can sometimes see moonbows, not rainbows.

Where's Clara?

1 Look and write.

| cloudy   rain   ice   sunny   snow   windy   rainbow   ~~cloud~~ |

1

.... cloud ....

2

....

3

....

4

....

5

....

6

....

7

....

8

....

2 Write the words in the correct order.

1 windy It's today .... It's windy today ....

2 sunny it Is .... ?

3 a rainbow is There ....

4 lots snow of There's ....

5 cloudy It is ....

6 are in There the clouds sky ....

7 skate on Let's the ice ....

3 Read and circle the weather words. Then match.

1

2

3

4

a

Dear Aunt Lily

It isn't sunny here, it's cloudy. There are big black clouds in the sky today. And there's lots of rain so it's very wet.

Love from Fred.

b

Dear Jane

I'm having fun in the mountains. There's lots of snow. Yesterday we skated on the ice on a lake!

Love from James.

c

Dear Lucy

We're having a lovely time. Yesterday there was a strong wind so we went sailing.
I love windy weather!

Love from Julia.

d

Dear Grandma

We're having a nice time in the countryside. The weather is sunny today. Yesterday there was sun and rain. We saw a rainbow!

Love from Sally.

4 Draw and write a holiday postcard. Describe the weather.

Dear ....

I'm ....

It's ....

There's ....

Love ....

5 Ask and answer with a friend. Guess the weather.

I'm swimming in the sea.

Is it hot and sunny?

Yes it is!

Review 2

1 🎯 Find the differences between the two pictures.

1

2

2 Match the words and pictures.

a e-book

b laptop

c pop star

d DVD

e bus station

f app

g send

h comic book

1
2
3
4

5
6

I'm at the bus station. Where are you?

7
8

3 Choose and write.

> countryside   kittens   sky   tractor   fields   ~~farmer~~   bats   plants

My uncle Fred has a farm – he's a ¹ farmer . The farm isn't in the city. It's in

the ² .... There aren't any shops but there are lots of big ³ .... where

the animals live. My uncle grows ⁴ .... on the farm too. I love riding

on my uncle's big red ⁵ .... I like all the animals on the farm too. My

uncle's cat had ⁶ .... last month. They are so cute! And there are lots of

black ⁷ .... that fly around in the ⁸ .... at night. They're cool!

4 Circle the words. Then write.

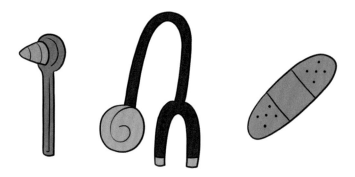

~~doctor~~hospitalliftseatdentistfall

1 This person helps people when you are ill. He's a ....doctor................. .

2 She can help you if you have toothache. She's a ....

3 This machine takes you up to the first floor. ....

4 This is something you sit on. It's a ....

5 It's a place where doctors and nurses work. ....

6 When you go ice-skating, you might .... on the ice.

5 (R2.1) Listen and tick.

1 [a]   [b]   2 [a]   [b]

3 [a]   [b]   4 [a]   [b]

Extra vocabulary

1. 🎧 (EV1) **Listen, point and say.**

| Monday | Tuesday | Wednesday | Thursday | Friday | Saturday | Sunday |

2. 🎧 (EV2) **Listen and say the day of the week.**

3. **Answer for you. Write.**

   1 What did you do last Tuesday afternoon? ....

   2 What did you do on Saturday morning? ....

   3 What did you do on Sunday evening? ....

4. 🎧 (EV3) **Listen, point and say.**

5. 🎧 (EV4) **Listen and number.**

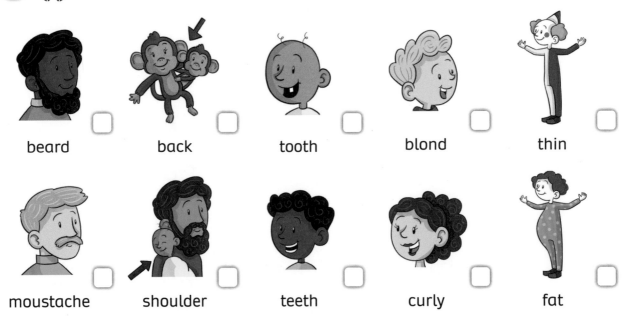

beard   back   tooth   blond   thin

moustache   shoulder   teeth   curly   fat

6. **Answer for you.**

   1 Has anyone in your family got ...

   a beard?   a moustache?   curly hair?   blond hair?